To:

Jokes, Cartoons, Quips & More

A daily dose of laughter for
good humor in your day,
to exercise your funny bone
and keep the blues away!

Inspired
by Faith

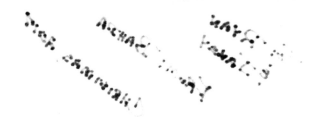

Jokes, Cartoons, Quips & More
ISBN 978-0-9963868-3-8

Published by Product Concept Mfg., Inc.
2175 N. Academy Circle #200, Colorado Springs, CO 80909

©2014 Product Concept Mfg., Inc. All rights reserved.

Contributions made by Carolyn Hoppe, N.L. Roloff, Patricia Mitchell,
and Vicki Kuyper in association with Product Concept Mfg., Inc.

Sayings not having a credit listed are contributed by writers
for Product Concept Mfg., Inc. or in a rare case,
the author is unknown.

Jokes, Cartoons, Quips & More

Laughing is the sensation of feeling good all over
and showing it principally in one spot.

Josh Billings

Want a good laugh? Then you've come to the right place. *Jokes, Cartoon, Quips and More* is a collection of one-liners, cartoons, jokes, and anecdotes, each one clever, clean, and completely sharable. Topics range from cars to kids, pets to personality, finances to family life, bosses to bargains and those everyday blunders that happen to us all.

Pick out a chuckle-a-day, or go page-by-page—either way, get ready to break into a smile. And if you're smiling, why not spread it around? With a kindly quip or a playful pun at the tip of your tongue, you can be the one who gives the gift anyone, anywhere, can use—laughter.

Truisms

The old believe everything, the middle-aged suspect everything, and the young know everything.

The shortest distance between two points is usually under construction.

Push will get you almost anyplace you want to go— except through a door marked Pull.

If the grass is greener on the other side of the fence, you know that your neighbor's water bill is higher than yours.

Curiosity is a wonderful quality to have— unless you're a cat.

The chance that you'll have food stuck between your front teeth is directly proportional to the importance of the occasion.

*Sometimes you've just got to go
after what you want.*

Question Me This!

If a pig loses its voice is it disgruntled?

When someone asks you, "A penny for your thoughts" and you put your two cents in, what happens to the other penny?

Why is the man who invests all your money called a broker?

When cheese gets its picture taken, what does it say?

Do Roman paramedics refer to IV's as 4's?

Why is it that if someone tells you there are 1 billion stars in the universe you will believe them, but if they tell you the plate is hot you have to touch it to make sure?

What do you call a fish with no eyes? A fsh.

If you dream in color, is it a pigment of your imagination?

If #2 pencils are so popular, why are they still #2?

If you jumped off a bridge in Paris, would you be in Seine?

Are you a natural-born pessimist if your blood-type is B-negative?

What three letters can change a boy into a man? AGE!

Things You Learn as a Kid

If you tell your mom something that makes her mad and she asks you, "Do I look stupid?" do not answer the question.

If you're in the principal's office for something, don't make a smart-aleck remark.

If your dad repeatedly threatens you with a punishment but doesn't carry it out, never tell him, "You always say that, but you never do it."

If you want something that your mom says costs too much, ask your grandma.

If you get a bad report card, show it to your mom when she's running late for work.

If you're going to do something your parents told you not to do, don't tell your little sister about it.

If you want a raise in your allowance, don't ask your parents at tax time.

Crossings

If you cross...

...a hen with a parrot, you'll get a bird that can lay an egg and tell you about it, too.

...poison ivy with a four-leaf clover, you'll get a rash of good luck.

...a malamute dog with a pointer hound, you'll get a moot point.

...a parrot with a lion, you'd better listen to the critter.

...a cow with an octopus, you'll get an animal that can milk itself.

...your TV with your microwave, you'll be able to watch an hour show in 10 minutes.

...a praying mantis with a termite, you'll get an insect that says grace before it eats your house.

...an alligator with a rose, it's unclear what you'll get; but don't bend down to pick it.

Marital Chuckles

While attending a marriage seminar on communication at their church, Lyle and Grace listened intently to the pastor who was speaking that evening.

The pastor explained, "It's essential that husbands and wives know the things that are most important to each other." The pastor then pointed to Lyle and asked, "Can you tell us your wife's favorite flower?"

Lyle leaned over to Grace, touched her hand lovingly and whispered, "It's whole wheat, isn't it, honey?"

"Wayne sensed the squirrels were becoming more aggressive."

For the Birds

Why does a chicken coop have two doors?
Because if it had four it would be a
chicken sedan.

Chickens are the only animals we eat before they're
born and after they're dead.

How did the pigeon get to the vet?
Flu.

Why did the turkey cross the road?
To prove he wasn't chicken.

Why did the chicken cross the
playground?
To get to the other slide!

How do you catch a unique bird?
Unique up on it!

Why did Mozart sell all his chickens?
They kept shouting, "Bach! Bach!"

Unhoppy News...

A woman brought her beloved rabbit into the vet's office for an examination. Placing the limp animal on the examining table, the woman watched the vet pull out his stethoscope and listen to the rabbit's chest.

"I'm very sorry, Mrs. Martin," he said sadly. "Your rabbit has passed away."

"That can't possibly be true!" she replied. "He was hopping around so happily this morning. Are you sure?"

"Yes, I'm positive," he replied.

"But you haven't done any testing," she said. "Maybe he's in a coma or something!"

The doctor rolled his eyes, then left the room. He returned a few minutes later with a Golden Retriever. To the woman's amazement, the dog put his front paws up on the table and sniffed the rabbit from head to tail. Then he looked at the vet and shook his head.

The vet led the dog out of the examining room and returned with a beautiful Siamese cat. He placed the cat on the examining table and it walked all around the rabbit, sniffing. Then it looked up at the vet and shook its head. The vet picked up the cat and left the room.

When he returned, he had a bill in his hands. "I'm sorry, Mrs. Martin, but your rabbit is definitely dead."

Mrs. Martin scanned the bill and said, "$200! How can it possibly cost $200 to tell me my rabbit has died?"

The vet reviewed the bill. "I'm sorry. I would have only charged $20 for the visit, but the Lab Report and Cat Scan were an additional $90 each!"

Tricky Tongue Twisters

The swan swam out to sea. Swim, swan, swim!

Some shun sunshine...do you shun sunshine?

She's so selfish she could sell shellfish shells, but shells of shellfish seldom sell.

**The big black bug bit a big black bear
and the big black bear bled blood.**

Can you can a can as a canner can can a can?

**Imagine an imaginary manager managing
an imaginary menagerie.**

Brisk brave brigadiers brandished broad bright blades,
blunderbusses and bludgeons—balancing them badly.

**Voted the most difficult by Guinness Book for World Records:
The sixth sick sheik's sixth sheep's sick.**

"I joined an on-line dating service
and said that I liked swimming and
formal wear. They've matched me
up with a penguin."

"ROOT VEGETABLES"

Newfangled Invention

An Amish boy and his father were visiting a mall for the first time. They were amazed by everything, but especially by two shiny silver walls that moved apart and then slide back together. "What's that, Father?" the boy asked.

The father, never having seen an elevator before responded, "I've never seen anything like it. I have to admit I don't have any idea what it is." While they were standing there, an elderly woman in a wheelchair rolled up to the moving walls and pushed a button. The walls opened and she rolled into a small room. The walls closed and the father and son watched the numbers above the doors light up sequentially until they reached the highest number. Then, the numbers began to light up in reverse order. When the numbers once again reached 1, the doors opened and a beautiful young woman stepped out.

The father turned to his son and said quietly, "Go get your mother."

Aging Isn't for Sissies

Three unmarried sisters, aged 92, 94 and 96 lived together in the very same house they'd grown up in. One night, the 96-year-old ran a bath. She put her foot in and then paused. "Was I getting in the bath or out of it?" she called down the stairs to her sisters.

The 94-year-old yelled back, "I don't know. I'll come up and see." She starts up the stairs and then pauses. "Was I going up the stairs or down?" she calls out to her sisters.

The 92-year-old who is enjoying a cup of tea at the weathered wooden table in the kitchen shakes her head and says to herself, "I sure hope I never get that forgetful, knock on wood." She then yells to her sisters, "I'll come up and help you both, as soon as I see who's at the door!"

Did you hear the one about...

...a fellow who plugged his electric blanket into the toaster? He spent the whole night popping out of bed.

...the new mother who asked her husband to buy a baby monitor? He looked and looked, but couldn't find one, so he bought her a baby Iguana instead.

... two meteorologists who fell down a flight of stairs? One broke both arms, the other broke both legs, and both couldn't stop worrying about the four casts.

...the small bunny who asked her mom where she came from? "A magician pulled you out of a hat," she said, "and I don't want to hear any more questions."

...the driver who was having trouble fastening his seat belt? It finally clicked.

...The do-it-yourselfer who wanted to learn about storage solutions for his home? So he went to the local library and asked if they had any books on shelves.

"I'd like to open a joint account with someone who has a lot of money."

Did You Hear That?

In the morning, a husband said to his wife, "That was quite a storm last night, wasn't it?"

"It stormed?" she said. "There wasn't thunder, was there?"

"Yes," replied her husband, "it thundered so hard that the house shook."

She held up her hands in dismay.

"Why didn't you wake me? You know I can't sleep when it thunders!"

After the Storm

After a tornado ripped across pastureland one night, a farmer called his neighbor the next morning to find out if his fences had been damaged. "Don't know," the neighbor replied. "Haven't found them yet."

Clothes Closet

A young boy opened the big Bible that had been in the family for several generations. He studied with fascination all the passages his ancestors had underlined, and examined the small, cursive notes crammed in the margins. While he was turning pages, suddenly a dozen dry oak and maple leaves fluttered to the ground.

"Oh, look, Mom!" he called out in delight. "I found where Adam and Eve kept their clothes!"

Something Special for You

A woman walked into a pet shop and said she wanted to buy a sweater for her dog. The assistant showed her a large display of canine garments, and the woman took her time examining several items.

"I just don't know," she said at last, "if I should take a small or a medium."

"You can bring your dog in and we can see which one fits the best," suggested the assistant.

"Oh, dear," said the customer, "I wouldn't want to do that. It's a gift, you see, and I want it to be a surprise."

Time Out

A man had worked long hours for weeks on end, and he felt he deserved a few days off. He knew, however, that his boss begrudged anyone taking extra time away from the office, so there was no use asking. He decided on another way to get what he wanted.

The next day he came into work as usual, but instead of sitting at his desk, he climbed on his desk, grabbed a ceiling light, and dangled from the fixture. When the boss saw him, he exclaimed, "What on earth are you doing?" The man declared, "I am a light bulb."

"You need a couple days off, buddy," the boss said. Agreeing, the man climbed down, got his jacket and left the office. Then the boss turned around and noticed his administrative assistant reaching for her coat and purse.

"And where are you going?" the boss shouted in exasperation.

"Home," she said.

"You don't expect me to work in the dark, do you?"

"He's fun, funny, handsome,
and a great
conversationalist...
but he's a tennis player,
and love means nothing to him."

Gotcha!

One morning, an elementary school teacher was running late for school. In her anxiety to make it on time, she was driving too fast and raced toward an intersection with a yellow light. Unfortunately, the light turned red just as she entered. A state trooper saw her, flagged her down, and wrote her a ticket.

When her court date arrived, she appeared before the judge and said, "Your Honor, I'm a good driver, and this is the first time I've ever gotten a ticket. I'm a school teacher, and I'm hoping I can attend traffic school instead of paying a heavy fine."

"School teacher, huh?" the judge said as his face broke into a huge grin.

"I've been waiting for an opportunity like this. You are to attend traffic school...and write 'I ran a red light and I will never do it again' 500 times!"

I refuse to accept I'm having "hot flashes." I prefer to believe my inner child is playing with matches.

Age Happens

A customer at a garden shop said to the cashier, "I'd like four of those pink flamingos, two giant pinwheels, three spinning sunflowers, one gnome and one of those bent-over grannies in bloomers for my yard."

The cashier responded, "That'll be twenty dollars for the flamingos, ten dollars for the pinwheels, twenty-one dollars for the spinning sunflowers, nineteen ninety-five for the garden gnome and an apology for my wife!"

In Good Time

Two elderly women were playing cards, something they'd done together for years. One day as they were playing, one of them said, "Please don't get mad, but for the life of me I can't remember your name! Please tell me what it is again."

The other woman glared at her friend, silently. Several minutes went by. Finally she said, "Uh, how soon do you need to know?"

How'd You Like to Live Here?
(Real Cities and Towns in the U.S.)

Bummerville, California

Constant Friendship, Maryland

Disco, Illinois

No Stop, Kentucky

Frog Jump, Tennessee

Fussville, Wisconsin

Goose Pimple Junction, Virginia

Mosquitoville, Vermont

Nameless, Tennessee

Puddle Town, Connecticut

Roaches, Illinois

Two Egg, Florida

Sweet Lips, Tennessee

Who'd a Thought It, Alabama

Zzyzx, California

Why, Arizona

How Do You Want That?

A traveler sat down in a café for dinner. He ordered the "budget steak," a steak at half the price. Yet when the traveler saw the waiter bring his dinner with his thumb planted squarely in the middle of the steak, he was appalled.

"Why is your finger on my steak?" he demanded.

"Sir," the waiter replied calmly, "you wouldn't want it falling on the floor again, would you?"

Knock, Knock...

Knock, knock. Who's there?
Elephants.
Elephants who?
Elephants Gerald...you know, the singer!

Knock, knock. Who's there?
Roxanne.
Roxanne who?
Roxanne shells were on the beach

Knock, knock. Who's there?
Deep.
Deep who?
Deep ends on who you were expecting?

Kid Stuff

"Class," the teacher asked, "Can someone give me a sentence about someone whose job it is to help keep people safe?"

Curtis raised his hand and said, "The fireman came down the ladder pregnant."

After class, the teacher took Curtis aside to correct him. "Do you understand what 'pregnant' means, Curtis?"

"Sure," Curtis replied. "It means carrying a child."

Sleepy Time

During a violent thunderstorm, Ryan's mother was tucking her little five-year-old son into bed. As she was about to turn off the light he asked, "Mommy, will you sleep with me tonight?"

"No, honey," his mother replied with a smile. "I need to sleep in Daddy's room."

As she closed the door she heard her son say, "The big sissy..."

Signs of the Times

Sign on a Jeweler's Shop:
If your watch doesn't tick, tock to us.

Sign at Whittler's Convention:
We don't care where the chips fall.

Sign outside Oceanography Class:
Open only to students who operate above C-level.

Sign at Maternity Hospital:
Welcome to the Heir Port

Sign on Vegetable Stand:
Take lettuce from the top or heads will roll!

Ditzy Definitions

Reality: that annoying time between waking up and internet access

Adult: person who has stopped growing at both ends and is now growing in the middle

Ukelele: Missing link between noise and music

Smile: a curve that can set many things straight

Vegetarian: a person who won't eat any animal that can be seen without a microscope

Avoidable: what a bullfighter tries to do

Cashew: the sound of a nut sneezing

Alarms: an octopus

Committee: a group of people who keep minutes and waste hours

Baloney: where some skirt hemlines lie

Egotist: someone who's always me-deep in conversation

Heroes: what a guy in a boat does

Giraffiti: spray painting very, very high

Donation: a country of female deer

Aftermath: the class following algebra

Tangont: a fellow who's been in the sun

Deja-stew: leftovers

Meanderthal: a very slow caveman

Lucille: aquarium escapee

**"We both went into
the dryer together,
but I came out alone!"**

Little Misunderstanding

Twelve-year-old Brian wanted to earn some spending money over summer vacation, so he started knocking on his neighbors' doors and asking if they had chores he could do. Mr. Pritchard, who lived three doors down was more than happy to help him out.

"I need someone to paint my porch," he told Brian. "I have the paint in the garage. You'd just need to do the work. How much would you charge for that?"
"Thirty dollars," Brian answered.

Knowing that he'd save himself some time and that he'd help keep Brian occupied, Mr. Pritchard hired him on the spot. He brought out the paint and a brush and handed them to Brian.

"I'll be working in the backyard," he said.
"Just come on back when you're done."
In what seemed like a relatively short time, Brian was at the back gate with an empty paint can.
"Finished!" he said proudly. "I even used the leftover paint to put on a second coat."

"Wow," Mr. Pritchard responded, "that was fast!"
"Oh, and by the way," Brian added, "It's not a Porch. It's a Lexus."

*"Archie, have you seen your
little sister anywhere?"*

Why Learning English Isn't Easy...

The farm used to produce good produce.

We must polish the Polish furniture.

The dump was so full it had to refuse more refuse.

The doctor wound the bandage around the wound.

When shot at, the dove dove for the bushes.

Who could object to the beautiful object?

She shed a tear over the tear in her wedding gown.

He could lead well if only he could get the lead out.

A helpful little tip from me to you:
Aways keep several get well cards
on the mantle. That way if unexpected
guests arrive they'll think you've
been ill and unable to clean the house!

Bumper Sticker Philosophy

INDECISION is the key to FLEXIBILITY!

TEAMWORK...means never having
to take all the blame yourself.

**Eagles may soar, but weasels don't
get sucked into jet engines.**

If you can read this, I've lost my trailer!

How do I set my laser printer to stun?

Two wrongs don't make a right,
but three rights make a left.

Location, Location, Location!

A group of psychology students from around the country were at an educational conference. In an "Emotional Extremes" class, the professor explained, "Before we get into the clinical portion of our lecture, let's establish a baseline for what we'll be discussing." He turned to a student from New York and asked, "What's the opposite of joy?"

"Sadness," she responded.

Next, he asked a student from California, "What's the opposite of depression?"

The young man answered, "Elation."

Then the professor turned to a student from Texas and asked, "And the opposite of woe?"

She replied with a smile, "I believe that would be giddy-up!"

**Sometimes you're the
windshield and sometimes you're...
well, you know.**

Men have got it made.
They get to DECIDE whether or not
they want to grow a mustache!

All In the Family

A woman walked into the kitchen and found her husband sneaking around with a fly swatter. "What are you doing?" she asked.

"Hunting flies!" he replied.

"Kill any?" she asked.

"Yup, 3 males, 2 females," he responded.

"How can you tell them apart?" she asked.

He responded, "3 were on the computer and 2 were on the phone."

Ridiculous Laws Still on the Books

In Altoona, Pennsylvania, it is illegal for babysitters to eat
the entire contents of the refrigerator while babysitting.

In Kansas, it's against the law to serve ice cream on cherry pie.

In Lynn, Massachusetts, it's illegal to give a child a cup of coffee.

**If you live in Saco, Missouri, you're not allowed to wear a hat that
will frighten a child.**

It's illegal to stop a child from jumping over a puddle in Hanford,
California.

**In Washington state it's against the law to pretend
your parents are rich.**

In Gary, Indiana, you cannot attend a theater production
within four hours of eating garlic.

**It's illegal on Sunday afternoon to play hopscotch
on the sidewalk in the state of Missouri.**

A kiss may not last for more than a second in Halethorpe, Maryland.

Leave It to Mark Twain

Mark Twain often told a story about how as a boy he sneaked up to a cart full of melons and stole one while the owner wasn't looking. Clutching his stolen prize, he ran off to a secluded spot, sat down and sank his teeth in it. But he couldn't swallow a single bite. Immediately, he made a decision. He sneaked back to the cart and exchanged the melon he'd swiped with a ripe one.

Leave It To Me...

I'm so broke that yesterday a pickpocket tried to pick my pocket and all he got was practice.

In school, I was so thin that when I stood sideways the teacher marked me absent.

My ranch is so big that when young couples go out to milk the cows, their grandchildren bring back the milk.

I'm so old that when I was a kid, rainbows were in black and white!

I'm so old that when I order a three-minute egg, the waiter asks for the money up front.

Real Rules of Conduct for Teachers in West Virginia in 1915

Teachers were not allowed to loiter at ice cream parlors.

They could not wear brightly colored clothing.

They were not allowed to date.

They were not allowed to dye their hair.

Unless they were at a school function,
they had to be home between 8pm and 6am.

They had to wear at least two petticoats.

They could not ride in a carriage or auto with a man who
wasn't their father or brother.

**They were not allowed to travel outside
the city limits, unless given permission
by the school board.**

Passing Through

Night fell when a hiker found himself out on deserted country road far from the nearest town. When he spied a farmhouse, he walked to the front door and knocked. As there was no answer, he went around to the back and tossed pebbles at an upstairs window. The window opened and the farmer leaned out.

"What do you want?" he angrily shouted to the stranger standing below.

"I'd like to stay here for the night," came the answer.

"So stay there for the night," the farmer growled as he slammed the window shut.

Now I See

A snake slithered to the optometrist's office and said, "My eyesight is getting so bad that I can't see well enough to find my way around anymore. Can you fit me with a pair of glasses?"

"Sure," replied the optometrist, and the snake returned to his home with a pair of glasses that gave him 20/20 vision. It was then he realized that the unfriendly neighbor who wouldn't even say "hi" was a garden hose.

Be Polite

Mom took her young daughter to the doctor's office to get a shot. As soon as the little girl saw the nurse pick up the needle, she broke into a loud wail.

"No! No! No!" she screamed at the top of her lungs.

"Now, now," cajoled her mother, "that's not what we say, is it?"

With barely a pause, the girl shrieked, "No, thank you! No, thank you! No, thank you!"

Where'd You Put Them?

While his son did his geography homework, his dad sat at the computer scrolling through his email. "Hey, Dad," the boy said, "where are the Andes?"

"Go ask your mom, son," he replied distractedly. "She puts everything away in this house."

LOST IN TRANSLATION:
Real Menu Items From Across the Globe

Menu item in Bali:
Toes with Butter and Jam

Menu item in China:
Fried Vegetarians Wrapped in Egg White

Menu item in China:
Cold Shredded Children and Sea Blubber in Spicy
Sauce

Menu item in Nepal:
Spaghetti Boneless

Menu item in Jakarta:
Chicken Mouse in Tartlet

Disconnect

Late one evening, a woman was awakened by the ring of her cell phone. Thinking it might be an emergency, she answered it groggily, without even checking the number.

A girl's frantic voice on the other end said, "Mom, this is Sherri and I'm sorry I had to call and wake you up, but my cell phone died and I had to borrow someone else's and let you know that I got a flat tire on Dad's car, but it wasn't my fault, honest, so please, please, please don't be upset, okay?" The tired woman replied, "I'm sorry, dear, but this is a wrong number. I don't have a daughter named Sherri."

"Wow, Mom," the girl replied, "I didn't think you'd be THIS mad!"

As I Suggested...

The overly confident golfer and his caddy were standing on the tee of a long par three. After surveying the distance, the golfer said, "This looks like a 4-wood and a putt to me."

His caddy politely suggested that he play it safe and hit a 4-iron and then a wedge. His ego bruised, the golfer growled at his caddy, informing him in no uncertain terms that he was equal to any pro and knew precisely what he was doing. So the caddy said no more and handed the golfer the 4-wood he had asked for. The player immediately topped the ball and watched in dismay as it rolled about fifteen yards off the front of the tee.

"It looks like it will be one long putt," the caddy commented as he pulled the putter out of the bag.

Groaners

What do you get when you cross a dog with a cell phone?
A golden receiver.

In which state is the Bay of Bengal?
Liquid.

What do you call a teenage girl who has
three boyfriends named William?
A Bill collector.

Why should you never argue with a doctor?
She has inside information!

What occurs once in a minute,
twice in a moment and never in a thousand years?
The letter M.

You Know You
Need Caffeine When...

If you spoke your mind you'd be speechless.

You eat instant coffee with a spoon.

**You put lipstick on your forehead just
to make-up your mind.**

When the barista asks how you
take your coffee, you answer, "Seriously."

Achoo!

A man woke up trembling with fear.

"What's the matter?" his wife asked him.

"I dreamed that I was in heaven," he replied.

"Well, that must have been a very pleasant dream, indeed! Why do you look so scared?"

"Because," the man said, "I was walking along, talking to God, and all of a sudden God sneezed and I had no idea what I was supposed to say to Him!"

No Change

An optometrist asked his new patient how long it had been since her eyes had been checked. "Oh, they've never been checked," replied the patient. "They've always been blue."

Remedy

A woman complained to her optometrist that every time she drank a cup of coffee, she felt a stabbing pain in her right eye. "What should I do?" she asked.

"My first suggestion," he said, "is to remove the spoon before you lift the cup."

Exercise for Couch Potatoes

To help tone those sagging underarms, here's an exercise designed for couch potatoes. Begin by standing on a comfortable surface, with plenty of room on either side to move your arms. With a 5 lb. potato sack in each hand, extend your arms straight out from your sides and hold them there for as long as you can.

Try to reach a full minute, then relax. Each day, you'll find that you can hold this position a bit longer. Repeat this exercise at least three times a week.

After a couple of weeks, move up to 10 lb. potato sacks. Then 50 lb. potato sacks. Eventually try to work your way up to where you can hold a 100 lb. potato sack in each hand with your arms straight out to the side for more than a full minute.

When you reach this stage, move on to the next level. Put a potato in each of the sacks.

Heaven-Bound

In church one Sunday morning, a preacher delivered a lively sermon on the glories of heaven. In conclusion, he shouted to his congregants, "Will everyone who wants to go to heaven please stand up!" Everyone rose from their pew except one man. The pastor noticed, and at the end of the service asked the man, "Are you telling me you don't want to go to heaven?"

"Of course I want to go to heaven," the man answered.

"Then why didn't you stand up when everyone else did?"

"Because I thought you might be planning a trip there this afternoon."

I Once Thought That...

**...it's a small world...but I changed my mind
the summer I ran out of gas in the middle
of the Mojave Desert.**

...I was always getting lost...but then I realized I simply
was discovering alternative routes.

**...I'd marry the boy next door...until my mom allowed
me to cross the street.**

...things improve with age...until I attended my 35th
class reunion.

**...I knew something about the law of gravity...but then
I started wondering how things stayed on the ground
before the law was passed.**

...I had gotten by with an illegal left turn...until I saw
the patrol car behind me doing the same thing.

Useful Knowledge

A college student worked part-time at a local pizza parlor delivering pizzas. One evening he had to go to the house of a woman notorious among the drivers for her skimpy tips. As he handed her her order, she said grumpily, "I suppose you would like a tip."

"Yes, ma'am, it would be appreciated," said the student, "but the other drivers told me that I'd be lucky to get so much as a quarter from you."

The woman bristled at the accusation. "Just to show you how wrong they were, here's $5!"

"Thank you, ma'am!" said the student, "This will go toward my college expenses."

"What are you studying?" asked the woman.

"Applied psychology," he said with a smile.

It's Fess-Up Time

One day in the grocery aisle, Jen comes face-to-face with one of her neighbors whom she knows fairly well. While the neighbor greets Jen by name and starts filling her in on all that has happened since they last met, Jen frantically fishes for the woman's name. Mary? Sue? Kathy? Or was it something more unusual? Like Meganna or Sherilynn... She keeps listening for a clue, but nothing the woman says jogs her memory.

Finally, Jen figures she can fake it with enough smiles and nods. And she does until a woman new to the neighborhood spots Jen and scurries over. "Would you mind introducing me?" the newcomer gushes.

"I'm so anxious to meet everyone!"

"All I had was a mild headache until I broke my wrist trying to open the aspirin bottle!"

Good Question

It was final exam time, and four off-campus college roommates were serious procrastinators when it came to studying for tests. The day before testing, they finally decided to crack the books, cramming until dawn, and then fell asleep exhausted, until 6:45 a.m. Trouble is, they had forgotten to study one of the subjects, and the exam for it was scheduled for 7 a.m. They quickly put together a plan.

They rubbed motor oil on their hands and wiped their hands on their clothes. Then they waited until the exam was nearly over, drove to campus, and rushed into the classroom. "We're really, really sorry, Professor," they panted, "but we had a flat tire on our way here and had to stop to fix it. Is there any way we can take the exam tomorrow?"

The professor calmly looked at the students, thought a few moments, and said, "Yes, I think that could be arranged. Come to my office tomorrow at this time and I'll let you take your exam."

They were delighted for the extra time, and leaving the classroom, they high-fived one another for having pulled off such a clever ruse. That day, they completed their other exams, went home, and spent the night boning up on the one remaining subject.

Returning to campus the next day, they appeared at the professor's office as instructed. He sat the four students in separate rooms, collected their electronic devices, and gave each one an exam consisting of two questions. The first question, worth 5 points, was easy to answer, and all four breezed through it. The second question, worth 95 points, read: "Which tire was it?"

Always refrain from giving advice to others.
They can't resist paying you back.

Truly, it is better to give than to receive.
It relieves you of having to send thank-you notes.

If you spend each day as if it were your last...
you'll be broke by nightfall.

Rest assured that lightning never strikes twice in the same
place. In most cases, the place isn't there anymore.

Live one day at a time.
That's the reason they come in consecutive order.

Insist that your children give you expensive,
high-quality gifts. That way, they won't inherit junk.

Things That Make
You Wonder Why

You've lugged dozens of boxes of family mementoes and collector's items through countless moves so you could pass them on to your kids. But now they're into the tiny-house movement and living in a space barely bigger than one of the boxes.

You're kneading bread dough and up to your elbows in flour, and that's when your nose starts running.

When you have only one hand free to unlock a door, the keys are always hiding somewhere at the bottom of your purse.

When you eat a piece of chocolate cake, crumbs fall all over the place; but all the calories gather in one place.

After all the new and improved pain relievers, we still have headaches.

The kids have been playing quietly for an hour, but the moment you sit down and get comfortable is when a fight breaks out.

Are We Having Fun Yet?

Have fun with people who enjoy arguing—agree with them!

The music student finally had a chance to conduct the school orchestra. He thought it was more fun than you could shake a stick at.

For his wife's birthday, a man bought her a belt and a bag to go with it. When his co-worker asked him how she like them, he said, "She wasn't very happy, but the vacuum cleaner works fine now.

A man stopped by a farmer's produce stand and bought an apple. "It's a pretty small apple," the buyer remarked as he paid for it. "Yep," the farmer replied.
Biting into the apple, the man exclaimed, "It's also sour!"
"Good thing it's small, isn't it?" the farmer replied.

You're sure to have fun at a theme park—
especially if you like waiting in lines.

Dad was teaching his daughter how to drive.
Suddenly she screamed, "Dad, here comes a utility pole!
What do I do now?"

One weekend, a husband and wife decided they'd like to get away from it all...so they loaded the car with children, snacks, pets, suitcases, toys, computer games, coloring books...

(Not) Par for the Course

A golfer decided to take his young son to watch while he played a round of golf, hoping to pique the boy's interest in the game. The round started out badly, however. On the first hole, Dad messed up his tee shot, had to retrieve the ball from a stand of dense bushes, fish it out of a muddy pond, and take several swings to free it from a sand trap. Finally, after half-dozen putts, the ball rolled to the hole and disappeared. "Oh, no!" cried the boy. "Now you'll never ever find it!"

Music to Your Ears

The bluegrass band member reached for his banjo, only to find that his banjo was weeping. The musician asked his banjo, "Why are you crying?" "Because," the instrument replied between sobs, "I'm tired of being picked on all the time."

A musician went into a music store and said she wanted to buy a violin. After being shown several and picking out the one she liked, the sales assistant asked, "Would you like a bow?" "No," the customer said, "you don't need to wrap it."

Did you hear about the pianist who kept banging his head against the keyboard? He was learning how to play by ear.

It's a Zoo Out There!

Out in the pasture, one cow was relating a lengthy story to another cow. When she was about halfway through, she noticed a young goat trotting over to them. "Oh, no!" the storytelling cow sighed. "Now I won't be able to finish telling you what happened without that kid butting in!"

A woman was walking her dog when she crossed paths with another dog-walker. Looking down to greet the new pooch, she noticed the animal was wearing spectacles. "I've never seen that before. How long has your dog been wearing glasses?" the woman asked the dog's owner.
"Ever since he was born," came the reply.
"He's a cock-eyed spaniel."

At an elephant-family reunion, the patriarch pachyderm started to address the crowd. His audience was all ears.

"Bored-er Collie."

Worry-for-Hire

The graduate accountant interviewed for a position at a small company. The interviewer, an anxiety-laden man, read through the resume and then turned his attention to the applicant.

"I see you have a degree in accounting, and that's what I'm looking for," he said.

"But just as important is having someone to do my worrying for me."

"Your worrying, sir?" the applicant said.

"Yes, in this business, there are so many things to worry about, and if money isn't one of them, that would be a real relief to me."

"I see," said the applicant. "What does the position pay?"

"I can start you out at a yearly salary of $105,000, plus benefits."

The applicant gasped.

"That's a very generous starting salary, but may I ask, how does such a small company afford that kind of compensation?"

"That," the man said, "would be your first worry."

My Word!

A woman carrying an easel, some paintbrushes, and a palette of paint was going door-to-door through the neighborhood. "Do you know what she's doing?" one neighbor asked another. "Yes," came the reply. "She's canvassing."

A surgeon had worked for years writing a medical textbook, but his editor rejected it. There was a problem with the appendix.

When his son asked if he could have a pet spider, Dad went to the local pet shop and asked how much it would be to buy one. "Fifty dollars," the clerk said. "That's outrageous!" Dad fumed. "I can get one a lot cheaper on the web!"

A man took his car to a garage for routine maintenance. Since earlier he had noticed that one tire appeared low, he asked the mechanic to check it out and add air. When the man went to pay the bill, he was shocked to see a $10 charge for air. "What is this?" he asked. "Air used to be free!" "Well, that's inflation for you," the cashier replied.

Have a Question?

Q: Which burns longer, white candles or red candles?
A: Neither. They both burn shorter.

Q: When is an eye not an eye?
A: When an onion makes it water.

Q: Why did the farmer plow his field with a steamroller?
A: Because he wanted to plant mashed potatoes.

Q: What did the painter say to his girlfriend on Valentine's Day?
A: "I love you with all my art!"

Q: How often do you rotate your tires?
A: Every time you drive the car!

Q: When does an elephant charge?
A: When it doesn't have the cash!

On One Hand

A boy arrived at school one morning wearing only one mitten. The teacher asked, "Jimmy, why do you have only one mitten?"

"Because I was watching the weather forecast last night," Jimmy replied, "and it said that today would be sunny, but on the other hand, quite cold."

It's a Deal!

On the first day of school, a teacher sent a note home with all her students.

"If you promise not to believe everything your child says happened at school," she wrote, "then I promise not to believe everything your child says happened at home."

How Should I Know?

A man went to the urgent care clinic and told the nurse that he had a bad wasp sting.

"Where is it?" asked the nurse.

Replied the man: "I don't know. It flew away."

Practical Matters First

"Doctor," the patient said, "I'm becoming more and more forgetful. I started out forgetting where I parked the car in parking lots, but now I'm forgetting where I parked it when I've put it in my garage."

"Hmmm," said the doctor. "Before we start treatment, I think you'd better pay me in advance."

Look on the Bright Side

A real estate agent was showing a prospective buyer a new home.

"I like to be honest with people," the agent said, "and I'm going to share with you not just the pluses of this property, but the minuses, too."

Looking around at what seemed to be a well-built and spacious home, the client said,

"So tell me what's not to like about this house."

"Well," said the agent, looking downcast, "across the field is a manure plant."

"I see," replied the client. "And what are the pluses?"

The agent brightened and announced, "You'll always know which direction the wind is blowing."

Let Sleeping Cats Lie

Two mischievous monkeys were sitting in a tree when they noticed a large lion ambling along the path beneath them. The king of beasts stepped off the path and stopped at the base of the tree, made himself a cozy cushion of leaves, stretched languidly, lay down, and fell into peaceful slumber. One monkey said to the other, "I dare you to go down and tickle that lion in the belly."

"I'll do it," the other monkey said. "I'm not afraid of that old fellow."

With that, the monkey stealthily scampered down the tree, tickled the lion's belly, and then ran off into the jungle. The lion woke up and angrily realized what had happened, so he decided it was time to teach the culprit a lesson. Springing into action, he dashed after the monkey. When the monkey heard the big cat gaining on him, he figured that he'd better act quickly or he would be caught in no time. Spying a newspaper that had been left lying on the ground, he picked it up, leaned against a rock, and started reading.

In a few moments, the lion showed up. "Say," he panted, "did you see a monkey run past you just now?"

The monkey lowered the paper and said, "You mean the monkey that tickled a sleeping lion in the belly?"

"I can't believe it!" cried the lion. "It's hit the media already!"

"Joe says we need to get back to nature, so he wants us to go camping a month this summer. But I told him, 'Joe, I love Mother Nature, too, but I don't see why we have to move in with her."

Amenity-Free Establishment

A traveler was checking into a budget hotel when the clerk asked him if he had a good memory for faces.

"Why do you ask?" the man said.

"Because there are no mirrors in the bathroom."

Rooms for Cheap

A traveler was checking into a budget hotel when the clerk said, "Rooms are $50 a night, $25 if you make your own bed."

"Not a problem," replied the traveler, "I'll make my own bed."

The clerk made a note of the guest's choice, and then handed him a hammer, nails, and lumber.

"For our anniversary, we went to that expensive nouveau cuisine restaurant downtown. After spending $200 on dinner, we got home, looked in the refrigerator, and realized that the babysitter had more to eat than we did."

Senior Moments

Two elderly gents were sitting on a park bench having a conversation. Suddenly one stopped mid-sentence, looked at the other and said, "Say, exactly what is your name again?"

"What do you mean, what is my name?" fumed the other. "We've been meeting every day on this same bench in this same park for fifteen years!"

The first man shook his head and said, "Yes, I know I should remember your name, and I'm really sorry. Could you please tell me again to refresh my memory?"

His friend sat silently for several minutes, lost in thought. At last he said, "So, how soon do you need to know?"

You Herd Right

Out in the field, two farmers were talking and the first farmer said:

"I've got a great flock of cows."

"You mean, 'herd' of cows," said the second farmer.

"Of course I've heard of cows," snapped the first. "I've got a whole flock of them!"

Get the Point?

A man came to work wearing a loud shirt and tie in a novelty print.

"What do you think of my new shirt?" the man asked one of his colleagues. "I bought it on our desert vacation, and it has different kinds of cactuses all over it."

"Cacti," corrected his colleague.

"Forget the tie," the man said, "look at the shirt!"

Thanks for the Information

A man had been stranded on a desert island for five years. Finally, he discovered a bottle with a note in it had been washed ashore. With trembling hands, he uncorked the bottle, unfolded the note, and read:

"Due to inactivity, we regret to inform you that your email account has been canceled."

Keeping Up with the Joneses

Bill took pride in his perfectly mown lawn and trimmed bushes. His neighbor, however, was a casual gardener, at best. One day Bill commented to the homeowner that an unkempt yard reflected poorly on the neighborhood.

"Look," the homeowner said, "my yard looks as good as anyone else's after the first good snowfall."

*"I decided I'd trace my family tree.
I never was very good at drawing."*

One Way

A man was strolling along the sidewalk when from around the corner came a crowd of people running toward him.

"Hey, what's going on?" cried the baffled pedestrian to anyone who would listen. Finally one of the runners slowed down long enough to shout, "A lion has escaped from the circus across town!"

"Which direction is he heading?" asked the pedestrian.

"You don't think we're chasing him, do you?"

As Excuses Go...

A long-distance trucker was driving a semi along the highway when he saw a sign that read, "Low Bridge Ahead."

Almost immediately, the bridge appeared right in front of him and he was traveling too fast to stop in time. He hit the bridge and got stuck, backing up traffic for miles back. When a state trooper arrived on the scene, he climbed out of his car, looked over the scene, and, with a jaunty air, approached the trucker.

"So," the trooper said, "looks like you got yourself stuck under the bridge."

"Not at all, sir," the trucker replied.

"I was delivering the bridge to a customer, and ran out of gas."

Did you hear the one about...

...the couple who met in a revolving door?
They're still going around together.

...the librarian who's expecting a baby?
Her colleagues are worried about her, though,
because she's two weeks overdue.

...the dieter who discovered that a
camera made her look heavier?
That's when she stopped eating cameras.

...the investor who put all his money
in a candy factory?
He made a mint.

...the lighthouse keeper who raised chickens?
He like to have eggs with his beacon.

...the dog that gave birth to puppies in the city park?
She was ticketed for littering.

Limited Resources

One day when Noah and his family were in the ark, Noah announced that he was bored and wanted to spend the day fishing. "That's a good idea," said his wife.

"Go ahead, and I'll see you at dinner."

So Noah picked up his rod and reel, stepped out of the ark, and began to fish. Thirty minutes later, he was back.

"How come so soon?" asked his wife.

"Aren't the fish biting today?"

"They're biting all right," Noah answered, "but I only had two worms."

Fish Tale

A father and son were out in a boat fishing.

"What's the biggest fish you ever caught, Dad."

"Son, I caught one once that was 14 inches."

His son thought about this a minute, and then ventured to say, "That doesn't sound like such a big fish to me."

"That's 14 inches between its eyes, Son."

Very Punny

A church janitor who is also the Sunday organist
always watches his keys and pews.

**Two geologists are examining a wide crevice left by a
recent earthquake. One turns to the other and says,
"It's not my fault."**

A sportscaster's wife just delivered twins.
The new dad was delighted with the infant replay.

**A newspaper reporter insists on wearing no-iron shirts,
citing freedom of the press.**

A shopper considers buying an origami belt, but then decides
against it because it would be a waist of paper.

**A CEO finally realizes that no matter how much she
pushed the envelope, it's still stationery.**

The Visitor

A man flew to a faraway country on business and was greeted at the airport by his friendly and affable host. Together they took a cab to the visitor's hotel, and at the end of the trip, the cab driver asked for ten dollars. Just as the visitor was about to hand over the cash, his host snatched it and angrily yelled at the driver in their native language. At the end of his tirade, the host handed the driver five dollars and scornfully waved him off.

As the cab disappeared around the block, the host turned to the visitor and handed him the rest of the money.

"Those cab drivers will rob you every chance they get. I apologize, sir."

"I understand," said the visitor, "but I think you should know that my luggage is still in the trunk of his cab."

Please Come Over

A stay-at-home mom was having a really rough day. The baby was restless and cranky, and her toddlers wouldn't settle down. She was behind in her housework, hadn't yet done the shopping, and was expecting company at dinner that evening. In the middle of all this, the phone rang. "Hi, daughter," a kindly female voice said.

"I just thought I'd check in and see how you're doing today."

"It's hectic, Mom!" And the harried homemaker proceeded to relate everything that was going wrong and all the work that had yet to be done.

"Let me help, sweetheart," the caller said.

"Give me half an hour, and I'll be over there to watch the kids and tidy up the house while you go to the grocery store."

"You're a lifesaver!"

"And I'll call John and remind him to come home early if your guests are expected at 6."

There was a pause. "John?" the homemaker said. "My husband's name is Bill."

Another pause. "Is this Tracey?"

"No, this is Shelley."

"I'm so sorry," the caller gushed, "but I dialed the wrong number! Please accept my apologies."

"Oh," Shelley said in a thin voice, "so that means you won't be coming over, I guess."

Life in the City

A woman goes into a bank in New York City and asks for a personal loan of $2,000. She tells the loan officer that she's going on a cruise for two weeks and would like to have the money in case an emergency should arise. As collateral, she offers the bank the car she owns, new-model sports car, fully paid for. She produces the title and keys to the car, and the loan officer extends the money. An employee drives the woman's car into the bank's underground garage, and the woman leaves on her cruise.

While she's gone, the employees at the bank take turns admiring the sleek and shiny car, chuckling among themselves as the silliness of using a $30,000 vehicle as collateral for a mere $2,000 loan.

Two weeks later the woman returns to the bank and repays the loan plus $12.50 interest. The loan officer thanks her for her business, but he can't keep himself from saying, "We see on your application that you earn a sizable salary and possess substantial financial assets. Why would someone in your position want to borrow $2,000?"

"I'll tell you," the woman replies, "there's no place else in the City I could park my car for two weeks for $12.50 and know it's safe and secure the whole time."

Occupational Wisdom

Acupuncturists take pride in a jab well done.

Parents are the ones who spend the first two years of their
kids' lives teaching them to walk and talk, and then the next
ten years telling them to sit down and be quiet.

Horticulturists are sure to grow on you.

Optometrists take a vacation whenever
the daily grind gets them down.

**The theater major had a reputation as a drama queen,
and she took it as a compliment.**

Mathematicians know what really counts.

Dentists are used to the drill.

On the Money

A tour guide was leading a group around Washington, D.C., when he pointed to a spot by the Potomac River.

"That's where tradition has it that George Washington was standing when he threw a coin to the other side."

"I don't believe it," scoffed one of the tourists.

"No one could throw a coin that far."

"You have to keep in mind," the guide said, "that money went a lot further back in those days."

Savings Plan

Because his young son was struggling in math class, his father thought he would offer the boy some incentive to do well on the final exam.

"If you get a good grade on the test," his father said, "I'll give you $50."

When test day came, the boy returned from school with a smile on his face.

"Hey Dad," he said, "you'll be glad to hear that I just saved you $50!"

Never Say No

The hardware store manager hired a new sales assistant. After he had been on the job for only three days, the manager overhead him tell a customer, "It's true, we haven't had any for a long time, and I don't think we'll get any in the near future, either."

After the customer left, the manager pulled the new-hire aside.

"Never tell a customer we can't get something," the manager instructed.

"You take down what they're asking for, and I can order it and have it here in a couple days—week at most."

The new-hire nodded and said he understood. Then the manager asked what it was the customer had wanted.

"Rain," replied the new-hire.

Young Love

A college student told his roommate that he proposed to his girlfriend that afternoon.

"What did she say?" asked the roommate.

"I don't know," the student replied. "She hasn't texted me back yet."

The Interview

A Human Resources manager was looking over an applicant's résumé. Turning to the applicant, she said: "Is there any skill you have that no one else has?"

"Yes," replied the applicant.

"I'm the only one who can read my handwriting."

The Jacket

Tom and his wife were cleaning out the basement one day when they came across a box of family mementoes. Rummaging through the contents, Tom happened on a dry-cleaning receipt from ten years ago.

"Now I know what happened to my favorite sports jacket," said Tom with a laugh, "I forgot to pick it up from the dry cleaners! I wonder if it's still there."

"I doubt it," his wife replied.

"Well, let's see, just for fun." With that, Tom put the ticket in his pocket. That afternoon, he went to the dry cleaning establishment and with a straight face, handed the clerk the ticket.

The clerk looked at the ticket and said he'd have to go in the back of the shop. After a few minutes, he shouted,

"Yep, here it is!"

"Seriously?" Tom called to the clerk.

"Who would have thought you'd have kept that jacket after all this time!"

The clerk came back to the counter.

"It'll be ready next Friday," he announced.

Name Game

A boy came home from his first day at school and said to his mother, "Mom, I'm so glad you named me Danny."

"Why is that, honey?"

"Because that's what the teacher and all the kids in my class call me."

It's True

A boy was sitting on the front lawn of a house. A neighborhood canvasser looked at him and asked, "Is your mother home?"

"Yep," said the boy.

The canvasser proceeded confidently up to the front door and rang the doorbell. No answer. After a minute, she rang the doorbell again, but still no answer. As she turned around and walked back to the sidewalk, she said to the boy, "I thought you told me that your mother was at home."

"She is," replied the boy, "but this isn't where I live."

Paving the Way

A woman wanted an attractive path through her rose garden, so she arranged for several hundred decorative pavers to be delivered to her home. She had never put in a path before and intended to find out how to do it, yet when the pavers arrived, she was so excited that she started laying them out right away. By early evening, the path was finished, but she realized that she hadn't prepared the ground and the pavers were uneven. So she took them up and put them in a pile next to her house until the next day.

The next day she raked the ground and laid out the pavers again. When she finished that evening, however, she decided that she didn't like the design, and she wanted to try another design tomorrow. Again she took up all the pavers and put them in a pile next to her house. The next morning, as she was relaying the pavers, a neighbor ambled over and said, "I see you're making a path through your garden."

"That's right," the woman said proudly.

"I was just wondering," said the neighbor, "are you planning on putting it away every night?"

Oops!

Instructions to ushers: "Seat late-comers in the back rows of the main floor or up in the baloney."

Society page: "The bride and groom exchanged wows in a garden ceremony."

Offer: "We will oil your sewing machine and adjust tension in your home."

Posted on the stage door: "Dancers: Tuesday, 10 a.m. Stress Rehearsal."

Announcement: "This month's event will include a DJ and balloons falling from the ceiling."

Note on the bulletin board: "Would like to trade a 5 x 8 loaf pan for an 8 x 5 loaf pan."

Ad in the newspaper: "Bad mitten set for sale - $25."

Free to Good Home: "Two kittens, one black and white, the other white and black."

Newspaper review: "The soloist offered three songs and a return to orchestral music was appreciated."

Store sign: "Blanket sale— these bargain lots are rapidly shrinking."

Second Time Around

Two country bumpkins went to the movies to see a Western. Toward the end of the movie, they watched as a cowboy astride a galloping horse headed straight for the edge of a cliff.

"I bet you twenty dollars he goes right over that cliff," said one.

"You're on," said the other.

Within ten seconds, the cowboy disappeared down the cliff. As the second man handed over the money, the first said,
"You know, pal, I feel guilty taking your money because I've seen this movie before."

"So have I," the second man said, "but I sure didn't think he'd be dumb enough to go over the cliff a second time."

Not Lion to You

At the zoo one day, a caretaker saw a visitor throwing $100 bills into the lions' enclosure.

"Stop!" the caretaker shouted.

"You'll make the animals sick!"

"The sign says it's okay," the visitor replied.

"It certainly doesn't!" the caretaker said angrily.

"I beg to differ," the visitor said, pointing to the sign that read: "Do not feed the lions. $100 fine."

Time on the Farm

A woman was visiting a farm. In the barnyard, she watched as the farmer lifted up each pig, one by one, so it could reach the apples hanging on an apple tree.

"Why don't you pick some apples and put them on the ground for the pigs?" she asked.

"Wouldn't that save a lot of time?"

The farmer looked at her incredulously and said, "Lady, time means nothin' to a pig."

Fair Warning

Big sister and her little brother were sitting together in church one Sunday morning. After about five minutes, little brother started squirming and giggling and even talking out loud. Big sister scowled at him, but that wasn't enough to improve his behavior. She leaned over and whispered in his ear, "We're in church! So be quiet and sit still!"

"Who's going to make me?" the boy retorted with an impish grin.

"Look back there," his sister said, pointing to the back of the church.

"See those two men? They're the hushers."

Cannot Tell a Lie

A little boy was growing up on his parents' farm located far outside of town. He loved everything about rural life, except for having to use an outhouse. It was cold in the winter, hot in the summer, and scary at night.

The outhouse stood on the bank of a stream. One afternoon, the boy decided to get rid of the offending structure by pushing it into the water. Since there had been heavy rain the day before, the stream was swollen, and the boy figured the outhouse would not have far to go if he gave it a few shoves in the right direction. So he shoved, and the outhouse tipped, rolled into the stream, and drifted away in the current.

That evening, his dad came into the boy's room and sat down. "Son," he said sternly, "It seems that someone pushed the outhouse into the stream this afternoon. Was it by any chance you?" Meekly, the boy nodded assent. He thought a moment, and then added, "You know, Dad, when George Washington chopped down the cherry tree, he wasn't punished because he admitted what he did."

"Yes, son," Dad replied, "but George Washington's father wasn't in the cherry tree."

Punny Stuff

An unlucky man sent ten different puns to a contest,
hoping at least one would win.
Sadly, no pun in ten did.

**What do you call someone who
used to be called Lee?
Formerly.**

What happens when seafood tries to dance?
It pulls a mussel.

**Two silk worms had a race,
but both ended up in a tie.**

How to Get Rich

"My philosophy," the successful business executive told a young graduate, "is always to do your best and give your best to your work, because it will bring you more satisfaction than getting a high salary."

Impressed, the graduate said, "Is that what brought you so much wealth?"

"No," replied the executive, "I became wealthy when I was able to convince my employees of that philosophy."

They're After Me

An employee went into the supervisor's office and said, "Boss, I need a raise in salary. And just so you know, there are four companies after me."

"Really?" said the supervisor.

"And may I ask which companies?"

"Gas, water, cable, and electric," the employee said.

Just a Suggestion

His team had not won a game for several seasons, and the coach was feeling depressed. Hoping to offer a helpful suggestion, a loyal fan said, "Have you ever gotten the team together for prayer before a game?"

"No, I haven't done that," the coach replied.

"There are so many things to pray about with this team that we'd get a penalty for delaying the game."

Worst Case Scenario

"Twenty teams in the league," the coach fumed to his players, "and you guys end up on the bottom at number 20."

"It could have been worse," one player timidly pointed out.

"How so?" the coach snarled.

"Well, sir, there could have been more teams in the league."

Uh-Oh

A boy knocked on his neighbor's door. When the homeowner answered the door, the boy said, "There's something of mine in your garage, and I've come to get it back."

Puzzled, the homeowner obliged, opened the garage door, and saw a baseball and a window with a baseball-sized hole in it. Looking at the boy, he said, "Now, how do you suppose your baseball landed in my garage?"

The boy looked at the ball and then at the window. "Wow, a perfect shot! I must have thrown it right through that hole!"

Mom...

A boy approached his mom looking quite sheepish.

"You know that vase you told me has been in the family for many past generations?" he said.

"Yes," his mom replied.

"The present generation just knocked it over."

*"When my toddlers act up,
I use a safe, comfortable playpen.
And when they calm down,
I get out."*

Here's Looking at You

On his way to campus one morning, a college professor stopped by his optometrist's office to pick up his first pair of bifocals. "You'll need to get used to them," the fitter said, "but after a few days if you're still having trouble, come back and see us." The professor took the glasses and put them in his pocket.

His first class that day was freshman history, and it was held in the auditorium to accommodate several hundred students along with the teaching assistants. The professor walked to the lectern and greeted the class. After arranging his papers, he pulled out his glasses, and began his lecture. He was delighted with how easily he could read the notes in front of him, but when he looked up, he experienced extreme dizziness. Midway through his lecture, he realized he was repeatedly putting on his glasses to read his notes, and then taking them off again to make eye contact with the students. He felt he owed the audience an explanation.

"These are my new bifocals," he said. "It seems that they're perfect for seeing what's right in front of me, but when I look out at you, I feel sick."

Get the Message?

Coming out of church one summer morning, a woman greeted the minister and said, "That was a marvelous message, Pastor. I found it so helpful."

"I hope you didn't find as helpful as you found my Christmas message," the minister replied.

"Whatever do you mean by that?" the woman said.

"Because that one seemed to have lasted you for six months."

Critic in Every Group

A pastor had hot-air hand dryers installed in the bathrooms of his church. The next month, however, he had them taken out. When a parishioner asked if the dryers had malfunctioned, the pastor said: "No, the dryers worked fine. I had them removed after I went into the men's room and saw that someone had taped a sign to the dryer that read: 'For a sample of this week's sermon, press here.' ".

Laughter's in the Air

After every flight, pilots need to inform mechanics if they've noticed any problems with the aircraft. When the mechanics fix the problem, they document their work on a form which the pilots review before taking off on the next flight. Here are a few actual maintenance requests by a pilot (P) and the response by a mechanic (M).

P: Left inside main tire almost needs replacement.
M: Almost replaced left inside main tire.

P: Something loose in cockpit.
M: Something tightened in cockpit.

P: Dead bugs on windshield.
M: Live bugs on backorder.

P: Evidence of leak on right main landing gear.
M: Evidence removed.

P: Suspected crack in windshield.
M: Suspect you're right.

P: Mouse in cockpit.
M: Cat installed.

P: Noise coming from under instrument panel.
   Sounds like a midget pounding on something
   with a hammer.
M: Took hammer away from midget.

P: Aircraft handles funny.
M: Aircraft warned to: straighten up,
   fly right and be serious.

P: Target radar hums.
M: Reprogrammed target radar with lyrics.

The Auction

At an auction, a man saw a beautiful parrot that he decided he wanted. He bid $25, but someone bid $30. He bid $35, but someone yelled out, "Fifty!" This went on for several minutes as the bids escalated, until the man shouted, "Two hundred dollars!" No other bids were heard, and the auctioneer said, "Sold for $200."

When the successful bidder came to pick up the parrot, he said to the auctioneer, "For such an expensive bird, I sure hope he can talk."

"He sure can," came the reply.

"Who do you think was bidding against you?"

Here to Buy

A man walked into a hardware store and asked the sales assistant for a bag of nails. "How long do you want them?" the clerk asked.

"Oh," said the man, "I would like to keep them."

Did you hear the one about...

...the romance in the tropical fish aquarium? It was a case of guppy love.

...the writer who announced he had written a best-seller? The only thing he had yet to do is find some best-buyers.

...the rocky marriage of the dentist and the manicurist? They fought tooth and nail.

...the woman who was asked by a passport agent to identify herself? She dug into her purse, pulled out a mirror, looked at it, and said, "That's me, all right."

...the staff member who asked her boss for more personal recognition? Her supervisor suggested wearing a name tag.

...the woman who went to an unfinished furniture store? They sold her a tree.

Accidentally on Purpose

A farm hand was seeing his doctor.
"Any accidents since I last saw you?" the physician asked.

"Nope," the farm hand replied, "nary a one."

"No cuts or bruises?"

The patient thought a minute and then said, "Well, last summer a rattlesnake bit me on the ankle. And then during a rodeo, a bronco kicked me in the ribs."

The physician looked at him in astonishment.
"Wouldn't you call those accidents?" the physician asked.

"No, doc," the farm hand replied, "I'm pretty certain those two ornery critters did it on purpose."

The Meter Reader

A utility company employee knocked on the college professor's door. When he answered, the employee said, "I'm here to read   your water meter."

"What's the world coming to!" exclaimed the professor. "Hasn't anyone introduced you to the classics?"

The Ad Was Right

A homemaker saw an ad in the newspaper for dishwashers at $100 each. "Hurry in!" the banner read.

"At this price, these won't last long!" Excited at the prospect of a new dishwasher, the homemaker rushed to the store and bought one. As it turned out, the ad was right—it didn't.

Proverbial Wisdom

The pen is mightier than the sword—
and much easier to write with, too.

**Life is what you make it—which could explain a lot of the
biographies on Internet dating sites.**

If you take the road less traveled, don't be surprised
if you soon will need new shock absorbers.

Sometimes it's best to swallow your pride—
and don't worry, it's calorie-free.

Sticks and stone may break your bones,
but words can never hurt you—
unless someone bops you on the head with a dictionary.

**You can't have everything—because if you did,
you'd have no place to put it.**

Practice makes perfect—
but then no one's perfect, so why practice?

*"I've never been overdrawn
at the bank!
Just under-deposited
from time to time."*

Diagnosis

A little girl came home from school one afternoon and told her mother that she had a stomach ache.

"It's just because your stomach is empty, honey," Mom said.

"Sit down and I'll fix you a nice snack, and you'll feel much better." Sure enough, after the girl had eaten her snack, her stomach ache disappeared.

That evening at dinner, Dad mentioned that he'd had a headache all day. The girl perked up.

"Dad," she said, "your head will feel much better after you put something in it."

Sound the Alarm

On the first day of nursery school, the teacher was telling her charges what to do in case of an emergency. She held up a smoke alarm and asked if anyone knew what it was.

"A smoke alarm!" the kids chorused.

"Now can someone tell me what it means when you hear this sound," the teacher said as she pressed the alarm test button.

"It means Daddy's cooking dinner tonight," a little voice piped up.

**The other cat says,
"Doctor, what are you
working on today?"
The first cat answers,
"My usual...String Theory."**

Confident Artist

Mom saw her little daughter with paper and pencil in hand and sitting at the kitchen table. Walking over to the table, Mom asked the girl what she was planning to draw.

"I want to make a portrait of God," the girl answered.

"Why, honey," Mom said with a smile, "God is invisible to human eyes. People don't know what He looks like."

Without looking up from her project, the girl replied: "They'll know when I'm finished."

Reason Why

A teacher asked her preschoolers, "Can a bear take off his warm winter overcoat?"

"No," the kids chorused.

"Why not?" asked the teacher.

Suddenly the room got quiet. Finally, one little voice piped up: "I think it's because only God knows where the buttons are."

All Right with You?

An OB-GYN had worked her way through med school by working part-time in a deli. The new mother couldn't help but notice when the physician delivered her first baby and announced, "It's a little over seven pounds. Is that okay?"

Not Yet?

One evening, a boy went to the hospital to visit his mother and his new twin sisters. On his way out, he stopped in an adjoining room where he saw a woman with her leg in traction.

"How long have you been in the hospital?" the boy asked the woman.

"It's been three weeks," said the woman.

"Then where's your baby?" the boy asked.

"Oh, I don't have a baby."

"You're sure taking a long time," the boy told her.

"My mom came in this morning and she already has two!"

The Invitation

A dentist was working late in his clinic one night when someone knocked at the door. When he opened it, a man said, "Can you help me, doc? I think I'm a moth."

"I'm a dentist," the doctor replied, "and you need to see a psychiatrist."

"Yes, I know that."

"Well, then why did you come here?"

"I was attracted by the light."

You can always pick out...

...the experienced mothers at children's birthday parties. They don't give each child a napkin—they sit all of them on drop cloths.

Remedy

A patient returned to the doctor's office for a follow-up visit. The doctor was puzzled when she saw that her patient's skin rash showed no signs of improvement. "Now you've been applying the ointment I prescribed every day for the past seven days, just like I said, haven't you?"

"No, doctor," the patient replied, "I couldn't. The instructions say 'apply locally,' and I've been out of town all week."

Help!

One morning, a man came into the emergency room.

"What happened?" asked the nurse on duty.

"I was in such a hurry to get to work," the man explained, "that I ran through my screen door and strained myself."

Truisms

You start cutting your wisdom teeth the first time you bite off more than you can chew.

Money isn't everything, but it is guaranteed to keep the kids in touch with you.

Laugh and the world laughs with you—cry and you have to blow your nose.

The person who says that nothing is impossible has never tried to eat an ice cream cone from the bottom up.

The grass is greener on the other side—but have you ever flipped it over to check?

One good turn gets most of the blankets.

If you can laugh when things go wrong, you probably don't realize what went wrong.

When the cat's away, no hair accumulates on the furniture.

"I love to lie on the beach.
Everyplace else,
I tell the truth."

Daffy-nitions

Electricity: Well-organized lightning.

Budget: A plan to live below your yearnings.

Hard-boiled egg: An egg that's hard to beat.

Carbage: Trash found in an automobile.

Experience: The positive spin we put on our mistakes.

Antique: A piece of furniture that has made a round trip to the attic and back.

Computer: A device that enables you to make errors faster than you could on your own.

Right Way

A boy is standing on the sidewalk outside a dress store while his mother shops. Soon the pastor, new in town, comes by and asks him where Main Street is. The boy points him in the right direction.

"Thanks, son, I appreciate your help," says the pastor.

"Now if you come to my church on Sunday, I'll show you the way to heaven."

"No thanks," says the boy. "You can't even find Main Street!"

Have a Question?

Q: Why are older homeowners so reluctant to get rid of all the stuff they've stored in their attics and basements over the years?
A: Because they know that as soon as they do, their adult kids will want to store stuff there!

Q: How do you get down from an elephant?
A: You don't. You get down from a duck.

Q: What did the French chef give his wife on her birthday?
A: A hug and a quiche!

Q: What did one raindrop say to the other?
A: Two's company; three's a cloud.

Q: Why didn't the skeleton accept the party invitation?
A: He had no body to go with.

Just Checking

A captain of an ocean liner observed the same ritual for 30 years: Every morning before appearing on deck, he would open his desk drawer, look at a piece of paper, nod, and then close the drawer. Upon the captain's retirement, his assistant, who was aware of the odd habit, finally got a chance to sit at the desk and open the drawer. On it he read: "Port left, starboard right."

Long Commute

An office worker's commute meant that he was on the road two hours in the morning and another two hours in the afternoon. When he complained to a coworker, the coworker suggested that, instead of the car, he take the train.

"That's not for me," the commuter said.

"I tried it once, and for the life of me, I couldn't drive the thing."

Long Vacation

"Vacations can last for months," the frequent traveler said to his friend. "You travel in August, return in September, get bills in October, get rested up by November, and find your luggage delivered to your door in December."

Fire!

"My house is on fire!" a woman reported to the fire department. "Please come quickly!"

"We'll be right over," the dispatcher said, "just tell us how to get there."

There was a pause on the line.

"Don't you have those big red trucks anymore?"

Be Quiet!

A small zoo couldn't afford to house a real gorilla, so they hired a man to dress in a gorilla costume and act like a great ape. So the man did, throwing himself into his role with abandon. Visitors laughed and clapped as he ate dozens of bananas, pranced around his enclosure, and thumped his chest dramatically. Then one day, trying a new antic, he accidentally flipped himself into the lion's enclosure.

"Help! Help!" he yelled in terror.

The king of beasts roared, lunged at him, put a paw on his chest and hissed, "Be quiet, or we'll both lose our jobs!"

Mr. Fix-It

Four engineers were carpooling on their way to an industrial complex when their car stalled. The mechanical engineer immediately diagnosed the problem.

"It's the pistons, guys," he said.

"Soon as we fix them, we'll be on our way."

"I think it's the spark plugs," countered the electrical engineer.

"All we have to do is replace them, and we're good to go."

"Bad gas," volunteered the chemical engineer.

"Let's flush the system, fill 'er up, and we're rolling." The three of them turned to the IT engineer, who so far had not said a word. He shrugged. "Let's get out of the car, slam the doors shut, open them, get in, and try revving it up again."

Problem Solved

"If our computers get too powerful," the programmer announced to his staff, "we'll organize them into committees. That will take care of it."

The Poet

A college freshman and a classmate, madly in love, were strolling along the beach. The young man gazed out at the water and declared with a wide flourish of his hand,

"Oh, sea, thou great and mighty force, roll on! Roll on!"

His girlfriend's eyes looked at him admiringly.

"Oh, Tom," she said, "you're so wonderful! It's doing it!"

Crazy for You

A sleek tomcat fell in love with the lovely calico next door.

"You're so beautiful," he purred in her ear.

"I'd die for you." Coyly she looked at him and said, "How many times?"

My Love

A girl asked her sweetheart, "Do you love me?"

"Of course I do, dear," he answered.

"Then would you die for me?" she probed.

"Uh—no. My love for you is an undying kind of love."

*"I took 'Introduction
to Shakespeare' last semester,
but it was really disappointing.
He never once showed up in class."*

How Come?

One day a baby camel came to his mom and said, "Mom, how come I have such large toes?"

"That's so, when you can walk across the desert, your feet won't sink in the deep sand," she answered.
The baby camel thought about this for a minute, decided it made sense, and then asked, "Mom, how come I have such long eyelashes?"

She said, "That's so, when you can walk across the desert, your eyes are shielded from the glaring sun and blowing sand."

The baby camel decided this made sense, too, and he asked yet another question, saying: "Mom, how come I have this big hump on my back?"

Mom smile and said, "That's so, when you walk across the desert, you can go for great distances without water. Isn't it wonderful how we're so well-equipped to travel comfortably across such a harsh landscape as a desert?"

"Yes," replied the baby camel, "but then, Mom, how come we live in a zoo?"

Difficult Jobs

One Sunday, the pastor's sermon lasted an unusually long time and little Kenny got antsy. When at last the service ended and he was in the car with his mom and dad, he said, "Is that all Pastor does is talk on Sunday morning?"

"Oh, no," replied his mother.

"During the week, Pastor visits shut-ins and people in the hospital, helps out at the food pantry, meets with families who need help, and makes sure that the church building is taken care of and everyone is happy."

"That's right," said his father.

"He also needs time to rest up, because speaking in public is not an easy thing to do." Kenny sighed.

"Listening isn't very easy, either."

Career Choice

Walking out of church one Sunday, a little boy announced to the pastor that he'd like to be a pastor when he grows up.

"That's wonderful, Johnny," the minister enthused.

"Now tell me what made you decide to become a pastor."

"Well, I have to go to church every Sunday anyway, so I figure it'll be more fun to stand up and do all the talking than to sit down and do all the listening.

"I told my kids that when it comes to Christmas presents, money is no object—unless what they want costs too much."

Did you hear the one about...

...the dog that flunked out of obedience school?
He blamed the kids for eating his homework.

**...the chemist who discovered a liquid
that would dissolve anything?
Trouble is, he couldn't find a container to keep it in.**

...the caterpillar that watched a butterfly flutter
and float on the currents of the wind? He promised himself
he'd never, ever get into one of those contraptions.

**...the fellow who heard that exercise
would add years to his life? After only 20 minutes
at the gym, he felt 15 years older.**

...the two dish antennae that met and got married?
The ceremony was boring, but the reception was excellent.

**...the recent grad who took an aptitude test?
Turns out he was best suited for retirement.**

"I told her getting a tan
was a bad idea,
but nooooo...."